SLUT

THE PLAY

☞ ACTING EDITION ☜

BY KATIE CAPPIELLO

In collaboration with
The Arts Effect All-Girl Theater Company

THE FEMINIST PRESS
AT THE CITY UNIVERSITY OF NEW YORK
NEW YORK CITY

Library of Congress Cataloging-in-Publication Data is available for this title.

This script is dedicated to
Helen Cappiello
and
Kay Goodwin.

CONTENTS

INTRODUCTION

In 2007, we established The Arts Effect All-Girl Theater Company to offer girls a supportive space to come together, train as actors, share their voices, and craft sharp, thought-provoking, feminist theater. Since then we've had the privilege of working with courageous ensembles of young artists and activists throughout the country and across the world, dedicated to exploring the realities of girl/womanhood and raising consciousness about the challenges girls face through theater.

We began developing *SLUT* in January 2012 in New York City through weekly creative sessions with The Arts Effect All-Girl Theater Company. During these sessions, the girls, twenty high school students from New York, New Jersey, Connecticut, and Pennsylvania, talked about the usual: dynamics at school, people they hooked up with at last weekend's parties, friendships on the rocks, pressure from teachers, aggressive boyfriends, and judgmental grandmothers. In the midst of all these conversations, we heard one word again and again: slut. "I mean, she's such a slut." "I felt like a slut." "I was dressed all slutty." "Haha. Oh my god, you're a dirty little slut!" The girls delved into heated discussions about how often and why they used the word slut to describe themselves and others. They determined that the word slut served as *the* barometer of female sexuality—the measurement of female status and self worth.

Sometimes through tears, members of the group explained (and occasionally reenacted) how they'd been slut shamed by girls, boys, women, and men for anything and everything: flirting with upperclassmen, lowerclassmen, or . . . *anyone*; "strutting" down the hallway; having large breasts; wearing a push-up bra; not wearing a bra; coming out as lesbian, bisexual, or transgender; being poor; being rich; being black; being Latina; being confident; being curious; kissing someone; liking sex; liking their bodies; posting a picture in a formfitting top; eating a popsicle; donning cutoff shorts, saying "vagina"; buying condoms . . . you name it. What stood out most: the girls revealed they'd been "slutted" after both consensual sexual experiences and experiences of sexual violence. In fact, a third of the girls shared details of their assaults.

What added to their frustration was the reality that the word slut functions simultaneously as a scarlet letter *and* a badge of honor. There's an attempt being made by girls and young women across the country to reclaim the word. Being a "slut" means you're sexy, fun, experimental, experienced, willing, popular, wanted, "fuckable," someone who parties, someone with friends, someone with power . . . and it means, most importantly, that you're not a prude. As one of our girls said, "The theory is if you can't beat it, own it . . . hey, sex isn't bad, being sexy isn't bad, so 'slut' can't hurt me, right? So I'll show them it doesn't hurt me by using it. The problem is, it can hurt you and it does hurt you. And it's just too hard to walk the line. Eventually you stumble or you get thrown down and any positive connotation disappears. Honestly, I can't think of another word that makes girls feel more degraded and worthless."

Then Georgetown student Sandra Fluke was called a slut by Rush Limbaugh for her support of women's access to birth control. Steubenville happened. Dominique Strauss-Kahn, the managing director of the International Monetary Fund (IMF), was arrested for sexually assaulting a female hotelroom attendant while visiting our city—she was subsequently attacked and accused of being a "hooker" by the *New York Post*. We watched the girls from New York City's Stuyvesant High School take on the school's slut-shaming dress code. Torrington, Connecticut happened. The brutal rapes in India and Cairo were all over the news, followed by the tragic suicides of Audrie Pott and Rehtaeh Parsons—teenage girls who had been raped, then brutally slut shamed by their communities. The devastating impact of slut culture was on full display and it felt more necessary than ever to give voice to those living this reality everyday, those we often don't hear from: the girls.

We hunkered down. Team members brought in stories to share and deconstruct. We held workshops and improvised countless variations of conflicts and relationships in hopes of discovering scenarios that best captured the complexity of slut shaming and sexual violence. Through reflective writing, we explored the different perspectives we aimed to incorporate. We and the girls talked to middle school, high school, and college students about their personal experiences as we developed the story line, characters, and dialogue to ensure the piece was authentic, nuanced, and hard-hitting. By January 2013, Katie had completed the script. It's important to note that everything in this play is inspired by real events.

In August of 2013, *SLUT* became an official selection of the New York International Fringe Festival and had its world premiere at The Lynn Redgrave Theater. To date, the girls have performed to sold-out audiences at theaters, museums, courthouses, coffee shops, art galleries, and universities throughout the country.

Our intention in creating and producing *SLUT* is to tell the truth—a truth that #YesAllWomen know too well. Brought to life by real girls, this play exposes the damaging language, shame, and deep-rooted sexism that fuel rape culture. While we don't believe *SLUT* preaches answers, we know it poses necessary questions. By "holding a mirror up to nature" and creating a live communal experience, something you can't turn off, log out of, minimize, or mute, we are determined to artistically ignite serious conversations about the effects of slutting on the lives of young people, the ways we all contribute to this culture, and what we can do to shift the tide.

Finally, we should say that this has not been the easiest process. While it has been rewarding in every way imaginable, we and the girls have experienced criticism, judgment, and anger. People questioned why we would let young girls take on such an intense issue. Is it appropriate to encourage girls to use offensive language and talk so openly about sex and sexuality? Why are you trying to shock people with the title and the dialogue? Is it healthy for a sixteen-year-old girl to portray a rape victim on stage? Valid questions. But, what's there to say beyond this: one in four girls will be sexually assaulted by the age of eighteen.[1] One in five college women will experience completed or attempted rape while in college.[2] Eighty-one percent of kids and teens experience sexual harassment during their middle school or high school years.[3] Clearly, it's time to talk about this, and young people are the ones living it. They are the experts. They have something to say and the stage gives them a place to speak their truths loud and proud, with no censor and no apology. Our girls will tell you, there is power in being part of the solution and they're motivated by a responsibility they feel to stand up for their peers. It's neither girls' nor theater's responsibility to be polite, appropriate, or cute. The goal should be truth, even if the truth makes people uncomfortable.

Inspiringly, for every bit of adversity, we've received an abundance of support. Thank you to the people of all ages from around the world who have courageously come forward with their own stories—vowing to no longer stay silent about their experiences with shame and violence.

We are very proud of the members of The Arts Effect All-Girl Theater Company and the StopSlut Global Coalition, the powerful activist community that stemmed from this play. Thank you for your bravery, strength, and leadership.

Thank you to the parents of our students for your trust and support; the teachers throughout the country who have introduced young people to this

1. Finkelhor, D., Hotaling, G., Lewis, I. A., and Smith, C. "Sexual Abuse in a National Survey of Adult Men and Women: Prevalence, Characteristics and Risk Factors." *Child Abuse & Neglect 14 (1990):* 19-28. doi:10.1016/0145-2134(90)90077-7
2. Krebs, C. P., Lindquist, C. H., Warner, T. D., Fisher, B. S., and Martin, S. L. "College Women's Experiences with Physically Forced, Alcohol- or Other Drug-Enabled, and Drug-Facilitated Sexual Assault Before and Since Entering College." *Journal of American College Health, 57*(6) (2009): 639–647.
3. *Teen Assault and Abuse*, Information Sheet (Wisconsin Coalition Against Sexual Assault: 2008).

work and given them a space to speak openly; the Feminist Press and Jennifer Baumgardner for believing in the power of *SLUT* from the start; Elizabeth Cuthrell, David Urrutia, and Jeremy Bloom of Evenstar Films for their passion, guidance, and creativity; Lauren Hersh, Yasmeen Hassan, and Equality Now for giving *SLUT* its first stage; Elena Holly and The New York International Fringe Festival; Daniel Melnick and Grant McDonald for their friendship, generosity, and incredible talents; the Smalley-Wall Family and Karen Stoker for getting this piece out there to new communities; Taryn Mann, Scott Yoselow and The Gersh Agency; our families and friends; our significant others Jamison and Jason and the audiences near and far who filled the theaters and started talking.

Action is desperately needed, and that begins with awareness and discussion. In our experience, theater provides the most effective platform for shared catharsis, the breaking of silence, and the cultivation of empathy.

–Katie Cappiello and Meg McInerney
Founders/Directors of
The Arts Effect

CAST

SLUT, by Katie Cappiello, presented by Evenstar Productions and The Arts Effect, produced by Elizabeth Cuthrell, David Urrutia, Katie Cappiello, and Meg McInerney, coproduced by Jeremy Bloom, production design by Grant McDonald, sound design by Daniel Melnick, lighting design by Gemma Kaneko, production stage manager Jenn Tash, directed by Katie Cappiello and Meg McInerney, had its premiere performance August 19, 2013, at the Lynn Redgrave Theater, NYC, with the following cast:

CAST
(In order of appearance)

JOEY DEL MARCO	Winnifred Bonjean-Alpart
CHRISTINA	Vikki Eugenis
NATALIE	Danielle Edson Cohen
GRACE	Casey Odesser
DANIELLE	Alice Stewart
JANE	Clare Frucht
ANNA	Eliza Price
LEILA	Willa Cuthrell
DOMINIQUE	Amari Rose Leigh
JULIE	Marcela Barry
SYLVIE	Samia Najimy Finnerty

The production was subsequently transferred to the Players Theatre, produced by Elizabeth Cuthrell, David Urrutia, Katie Cappiello, and Meg McInerney, coproduced by Jeremy Bloom, on September 14, 2013.

Pop-up productions, produced by Elizabeth Cuthrell, David Urrutia, Katie Cappiello, and Meg McInerney, coproduced by Jeremy Bloom, were held at the following locations: The Hammer Museum's Billy Wilder Theater in Los Angeles, presented by Equality Now and the Smalley-Wall family, premiered on April 27, 2014; North Dakota State University and Ecce Art Gallery in Fargo, North Dakota, presented by the Feminist Press and Karen Stoker, premiered on May 1, 2014; the Gym at Judson in New York City premiered on May 10, 2014. Technical design for pop-up productions was led by Daniel Melnick with lighting design by Alejandro Fajardo (NYC); stage managers were Janelle Richardson (LA), Laurie Seifert Williams (Fargo), and Niki Armato (NYC). The casts were as follows:

JOEY DEL MARCO	Winnifred Bonjean-Alpart
CHRISTINA	Vikki Eugenis
NATALIE	Danielle Edson Cohen (LA, NYC) India Witkin (Fargo)
GRACE	Casey Odesser
DANIELLE	Alice Stewart
JANE	Clare Frucht (LA, NYC) Maya Blake (Fargo)
ANNA	Eliza Price
LEILA	Willa Cuthrell (LA, NYC) Bella Danieli (Fargo)
DOMINIQUE	Amari Rose Leigh (LA, NYC) Darci Siegel (Fargo)
JULIE	Marcela Barry
SYLVIE	Samia Najimy Finnerty (LA, NYC) Mary Louise Miller (Fargo)

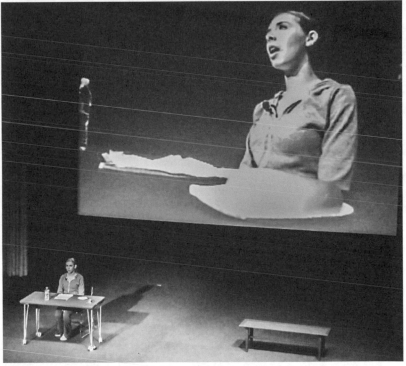

Scenes from the Los Angeles production of *SLUT*. Design by Daniel Melnick and Grant McDonald. Photographs by Barbara Katz.

CHARACTERS

JOEY: High school junior, 16.

CHRISTINA: High school junior, 16, member of "the Slut Squad."

NATALIE: High school junior, 16, member of "the Slut Squad."

GRACE: High school sophomore, 15, member of "the Slut Squad."

DANIELLE: High school freshman, 14, new member of "the Slut Squad."

JANE: High school junior, 16, Joey's best friend.

ANNA: High school junior, 16, Joey's close friend, twin sister of Tim.

LEILA: High school freshman, 14, Danielle's best friend,
    "dating" George.

DOMINIQUE: High school junior, 16, a schoolmate of Joey's,
    different social circle.

JULIE: High school junior, 17, a schoolmate of Joey's,
    different social circle.

SYLVIE: High school junior, 16, an acquaintance of Joey's.

TIME
Winter, present day.

PLACE
New York City.

SLUT

THE PLAY

PROLOGUE: PREGAMING

I

SCENE: *The stage is simply set with a screen centered on the back wall. A table and chair are stage right, and a bench or two black boxes are stage left to be used for any of the play's scenes. A water bottle, bottle of vodka, computer, five gym bags, and clothes are set on the stage. An image of a locker room is projected on the screen. It's dark, with only a harsh overhead florescent light shining on JOEY, who stands center stage. JOEY looks straight out into the audience, sweaty, in shorts and a sports bra. It's dead silent until the other members of the Elliot Dance Team enter. CHRISTINA, NATALIE, and GRACE burst onto the stage enthusiastically, talking up a storm, dancing around, exhausted from practice. Joey is pulled into the scene. Because she is a freshman, DANIELLE stands in the doorway to the locker room, waiting for the upperclassmen to clear out before she's allowed to enter. NATALIE looks in the locker-room mirror as she tries to get today's dance sequence just right. GRACE, CHRISTINA, and JOEY begin to change into sweats.*

CHRISTINA. (*To* NATALIE.) No—no, no, no. Wait. Stop—stop! That's not it. What are you doing? It's this. Okay—it's one-two-three-and-push-and-five-six-kick-seven-and-eight. (CHRISTINA *shows* NATALIE *the dance sequence.*) Yeah. The kick is on the offbeat. (NATALIE *does it again.*) No! (*The* GIRLS *burst into laughter.*) Forget it. Dude, you suck at that shit.

NATALIE. I don't even care. (*She lets out a massive scream.*) I'm so tired! My legs are killing me. What's up with all the squats in warm-up now? PS, did you guys see me trip before my aerial?

CHRISTINA. Yes, and it was amazing. Ms. Miller was just *not* having you today!

NATALIE. I know! . . . I'm a disaster. I'm just so freakin' tired. This week just straight up killed me.

JOEY. Want this? (*She pulls a Red Bull out of her bag, cracks it open, has a sip, and passes it around.*)

NATALIE. Yeah. (GRACE *grabs it before* NATALIE *has a chance.*)

GRACE. (*Takes a sip.*) Ugh—fucking nasty. (NATALIE *grabs it.*)

NATALIE. (*Mockingly.*) Oh my god, Gracie! I'm so sorry we didn't bring any vodka to water it down for ya!

GRACE. (*Mockingly back.*) Oh my god, Natalie, you're just so hilar!

CHRISTINA. Okay, what's everyone wearing to Connor's?

JOEY. I don't know.

GRACE. Lace tank top from Urban, red velvet skirt, don't know what shoes.

NATALIE. My miniskirt thing that's made out of sweater material, no tights, with my mom's Dolce Vita little black booties.

CHRISTINA. Don't call them booties, it sounds weird.

JOEY. Oh! So agree! Like panties—panties and booties are so, like, dainty and, like . . . uh—

CHRISTINA. Victorian, or puritanical, or something.

JOEY. Yes! They sound oddly, like, perverted to me.

NATALIE. Okay. Wow. My mom's Dolce Vita *ankle boots*. How's that for ya? Oh, JoJo, I wanted to ask you, can I borrow your AP World History notes please?

JOEY. Definitely. Here. (*She tosses the notebook to* NATALIE.) You wanna study on Sunday?

NATALIE. Yes please! Hey, do you think your parents will care if we do your house and then your dad can make us pizza? I'm going to carb my ass off.

GRACE. Ugh!! (*She's been examining her upper-inner thigh.*)

NATALIE. What?

GRACE. Fuck!

CHRISTINA. What?

GRACE. Look at this shit. (*She shows everyone her inner thigh.*)

JOEY. Oooff—looks like you got a little chub rub going on there, Gracie.

GRACE. What? I do not. But seriously, what is it? It's like a rash-type thing.

DANIELLE. It's definitely chub rub.

GRACE. (*Kind of jokingly.*) Dude! Dani, why the fuck are you talking? Keep your freshman mouth closed.

NATALIE. It's chub rub.

3

GRACE. But I'm, like, not fat, am I? And I've never had it before. Wouldn't I have had it before? How is this possible?

NATALIE. Your sexy thighs were smacking against each other during laps or something.

GRACE. It hurts . . .

JOEY. No kidding! You gotta slather Vaseline all over your inner thighs next practice.

GRACE. Does it look that bad? Does it look like it's a cluster of sores or something? Does it look like I have the herps?

NATALIE. Yup. Definitely. Looks just like herpes.

JOEY. You would know.

NATALIE. Thanks!

JOEY. Anytime!

CHRISTINA. (*To* GRACE.) Wow, no one is gonna hook up with you again.

JOEY. Like, ever again. This is a sad day for you, Gracie.

NATALIE. You and George tonight—not happening now, no matter how hot he thinks you are.

GRACE. First of all, I've moved on from George, thank you; and you would know that if you had actually listened to me in chem today. He's hooking up with Annoyingly Cute Freshman Girl. So fuck you, Nat. Second of all, I'm just gonna say two words: Bloody Beaver.

NATALIE. What?

GRACE. Yeah. I'm gonna be the next fucking *Bloody Beaver*.

JOEY. Oh my god, Grace! (*To* NATALIE.) Bloody Beaver. You don't remember that? Hunter Gaynes got everyone calling Nadia Boyd that after they hooked up.

CHRISTINA. Right, right, yes! Yes, okay, but, like, how dumb is she, though? You don't let a guy hook up with you when you have your period. Is she retarded?

JOEY. Don't.

CHRISTINA. Sorry. Is she mentally challenged? God. Anyway, this is not a Bloody Beaver situation Gracie, okay?

JOEY. Yeah, it's definitely not. But for the record, Hunter is a little freshman douche. He put that shit all over Facebook. Fuck him, man. She's like—how even old is she, Dani?

DANIELLE. She's fourteen, but she was thirteen at the time.

JOEY. And it was the first time she ever really hooked up. I mean, she didn't know what to do.

NATALIE. And she's so cute. I love her.

JOEY. Oh, love her.

NATALIE. And she, like, loves us. We should tell all the freshman girls not to hook up with him. Seriously.

JOEY. Yes.

NATALIE. Danielle, tell them. (DANIELLE *gestures in agreement and smiles.*)

GRACE. Hey, hey, hey—what if I wear tights? The ones with the seam up the back so they still look really cute.

NATALIE. Well, considering your drunken strip-tease last weekend, you'll probably end up taking them off anyway, so—

GRACE. Whatever Nat. Jealous? Of my *sex-ay* moves?

NATALIE. Oh, yeah. I'm jealous of *you*, with your chub rub, for sure. Hate to say it Gracie, but that's it for you dude. Sorry. You're a herpes-ridden dirty slut now so—

GRACE. I'm gonna kill you, Natalie. And you should just shut it because you are the biggest . . . dirtiest . . . sluttiest slut of, like, all time. (GRACE *laughs—the following banter is routine for these girls.*)

NATALIE. Hell yeah, I am. Jealous?

JOEY. Okay, no way is she the biggest slut of the Slut Squad! I can slut it up with the sluttiest of y'all, thank you very much! Including Natalie.

CHRISTINA. Hey!

NATALIE. Ohhhh Chrissy! You know we respect your sexy slutness. (NATALIE *digs though her makeup bag.*)

CHRISTINA. You better. And don't make me challenge you to a slut-off.

NATALIE. (*To* GRACE.) Okay, let me see it again. Here. (NATALIE *begins to cover* GRACE'S *rash with concealer and powder.*)

CHRISTINA. 'Cause you'll go down bitches. 'Cause I'll just walk right up to Derek Walker and—

NATALIE. (*Referring to* GRACE'S *crotch.*) Okay, check it out! Look. It's not that bad now, right? I just covered it with concealer and powder. Look.

GRACE. Is it okay? (*They all look at* GRACE'S *thigh.*) Is it crusty? It's totally crusty, right? I'm gonna have a fucking crusty crotch at this party!

JOEY. Grace, it's fine. We're messing with you. Any guy of your choosing will still wanna get all up on your shit and no one is gonna say anything.

GRACE. Okay.

JOEY. And you wanna know why?

GRACE. 'Cause I'm a sexy mama and you love me?

NATALIE. Yep. *And* you don't mess with Slut Squad girls. Because we will take you down, motherfucker.

CHRISTINA. Awww, Slut Squad love!

GRACE. Slut Squad crazy love!

NATALIE. (*Chugs the last of the Red Bull and jumps up on the locker-room bench.*) Slut Squad crazy, mad, stupid love! (*The girls break into their chant, the team anthem. It's goofy and fun, but they kind of mean it . . .*) S-L-U-T S-Q-U-A-D!

ALL.
YES, THAT'S WHO WE BE.

NATALIE.
SAY WHAT?

ALL.
YES, THAT'S WHO WE BE.
AND, BITCHES, WE GO DOWN LIKE NO OTHER GIRLS IN TOWN.
AND WHEN WE STRUT THROUGH THE SCHOOL,
YOU KNOW WE MAKE THEM BOYS DROOL.
BECAUSE THEY ALL WANNA PIECE OF THIS.
AND YOU KNOW YOU CAN'T SLUT LIKE THIS.
HIS ANACONDA DON'T WANT NONE
BECAUSE YOU AIN'T ME, SON! OH YES.
OUR MILKSHAKE BRINGS ALL THE BOYS TO THE YARD.
AND THEY'RE, LIKE, IT'S BETTER THAN YOURS.
DAMN RIGHT! IT'S BETTER THAN YOURS.
COULD WE TEACH YOU? HELL NO!

(CHRISTINA, NATALIE, *and* GRACE *exit with all their stuff, joking, dancing, having fun.* DANIELLE *enters and crosses, trying not to get in* JOEY's *way, and exits to the showers. Lights fade to black.*)

II

SCENE: *Music is playing as* JOEY *gets ready for the party. She checks herself in the mirror and digs through her clothes while dancing around. She is alerted to a video chat coming through on the computer. She rushes to turn down the music and answer the call. Her best friend* JANE *pops up as a video on the projection screen.*

JOEY. Hey!

JANE. Hey!

JOEY. Do you like this lipstick?

JANE. Yeah.

JOEY. How was track?

JANE. Well apparently, I'm slow now, which is frustrating.

JOEY. Oh! Okay, so Gracie has a rash near her crotch. So, the door is open for you with George tonight!

JANE. Oh please, and what? Be, like, the hundredth girl he's hooked up with this year? He's hot, but I don't wanna be one of his, like, bevy of sluts. And isn't he hooking up with Annoyingly Cute Freshman Girl?

JOEY. Yeah, but whatever. (JOEY *continues to dress for the party.*) You're going to come to Luke's with me right?

JANE. I can't. My mom is making me eat here.

JOEY. You know your mom's just banning you from going because Linda's a Republican.

JANE. (*Laughing.*) Yeah probably! She fucking hates Linda. That's why she didn't want me going out with Luke, remember? She was all like, "Janey, hey, if you wanna go out with some kid whose mother thinks it's still nineteen-fucking-fifty, go right ahead. But I'm just warning you, if you get pregnant that woman will be your worst fucking nightmare."

JOEY. (*Laughing.*) Your mom's hilarious.

JANE. Yeah. Who's going to Luke's?

JOEY. (*Putting on shoes.*) Luke, George, me, Anna . . . (*teasingly*) and Tim.

JANE. Shut up. Do you think Anna hates me because I want to hook up with her brother?

JOEY. No.

JANE. I like Tim. He's the only one of those three that's not a dick.

JOEY. Oh, come on! That's not true. George is not a dick. And Luke is just an idiot. (*She is now fully dressed.*) Okay. What do you think? (*Shows her outfit to* JANE.) Too slutty?

JANE. No, it's perfect.

JOEY. I love you. Hey, you wanna sleep over tonight?

JANE. Yeah!

JOEY. My parents will be so excited. They seriously think we're still twelve when we have sleepovers.

JANE. Ha! Funny. Okay, dinnertime. See you later. Love you. Bye.

JOEY. K. Love you. Bye.

(*Screen goes dark.* JOEY *turns the music back on and begins to work on her hair. Again, her video chat begins to ring. She pauses the music and answers.* ANNA *pops up as video on the projection screen.*)

JOEY. Hola!

ANNA. Hey! I can't really talk, but I wanted to video chat you for a quick sec. I'm grounded and they took my phone. I'm sure they're gonna take my computer, too, but I wanted to tell you that I can't come tonight, okay?

JOEY. No! Are you serious? What did you do?

ANNA. Thea was driving me crazy. She wore my sweater to school today and got shit on it. And then she was being all up in my shit from the minute I got home. So I just smashed her in the face. (*They laugh.*) And she, like, threw a shit-fit and my parents went off the deep end at me. So I'm grounded . . . which is really annoying because she totally deserved it, and honestly, I can kinda tell my mom thinks so, too, because she said I can still watch TV.

JOEY. Sucks. I'm gonna murder Thea.

ANNA. Right? She's such a stupid little whore. She's becoming a real bitch, too.

JOEY. She's eleven!

ANNA. (*Hearing her mom coming up the stairs.*) Hey, I really gotta go, but I won't have my phone FYI so . . . or probably this computer so . . . have fun. I'm so jealous! I hate myself right now. Okay, bye.

JOEY. Wait!

ANNA. What?

JOEY. Tim's still coming right?

ANNA. Yeah, yeah. He told me to tell you. He's the current "good child" of the family. Thea and I are fuckups but Timmy's perfect. Have so much fun. Take care of my brother. Keep him away from the ratchet hos, please!

JOEY. (*Laughing.*) Yes! Okay, bye. Love you. Go read something.

ANNA. No way. *Friday Night Lights* marathon.

JOEY. OOOOooo. Tim Riggins!

ANNA. My dream man. I wanna do him.

JOEY. Ha! Love you. Bye.

ANNA. Love you. Bye.

(*Screen goes dark.* JOEY *turns on the music. She looks at herself in the mirror, satisfied. The music changes, she begins to dance. Lights dim and a spotlight focuses on* JOEY *as images (photos/video) of the action are projected on the screen. First are images of* JOEY *pregaming at* LUKE'S *house, having fun, laughing. Onstage* JOEY *sings along to the song and drinks vodka from the bottle; she appears to be getting drunk. The projections and music segue into the sights and sounds of a busy New York street. Onstage* JOEY *is freezing, shaking to keep warm, clearly tipsy, while looking for a taxi. She rushes across the stage, flagging down a taxi.*)

JOEY. You guys, I got one. Let's go. Someone's gotta sit in the front. No, seriously, we're not gonna fit. Someone should sit in the front next to, um, him, um—what's your name, sir? . . . Apunda! Someone's gotta sit next to my friend Apunda up front, okay? Fine. We'll just squish—get in—I'm freezing! Apunda, we're going to Park and 89th.

(*Sound of taxi door slamming shut. The music suddenly stops and the screen goes dark. The same harsh overhead light from the opening of the play shines on* JOEY. *She stands there, dead silent, trying to catch her breath. She turns and violently vomits. Lights slowly come up. Muffled music plays from the other room. Photos of the party are projected on the screen.* JOEY *is in the bathroom; she sinks to the floor. After a moment, she turns to vomit again. She wipes her mouth and tries to breathe. She takes her cell phone out of her bag. There's a knock on the bathroom door.*)

JANE. (*Offstage.*) Jo, are you okay? (*Another knock.*) Joey, let me in, okay? Come on, it's me. Open the fucking door. Are you okay? (JOEY *gets up and shakily opens the door. The music volume increases for a moment as the door opens.* JOEY *sits down near the door.* JANE *enters and locks the door behind her.*)
JANE. Dude, are you okay? You look like shit. Did you throw up? (JOEY *nods her head yes—and suddenly turns and vomits again.* JANE *rushes to hold her hair back.*) Are you okay? Are you just really fucked up?
JOEY. (*Barely able to talk.*) I'm such a slut. (*She tries to breathe.*)

(*Music fades and lights dim. Spotlight on* JOEY *and* JANE *as* JOEY *begins to remove her makeup and* JANE *helps her into sweatpants and a zip-up sweatshirt. The spotlight fades to black.*)

SCENE 1. WHERE DO I START?

SCENE: *Lights up on* JOEY, *sitting at a table downstage right. The rest of the stage is dark. She is being interviewed by the Assistant District Attorney.*

JOEY. You're going to record what I say? . . . Okay . . . should I just start or—Okay. Um, Joanna Grace Del Marco. I'm sixteen years old. I live at 535 East 14th Street, apartment 8F, 10009. That's in Stuyvesant Town . . . What? Oh, okay. Yes, sure, okay. Yeah, I understand, okay. I am agreeing to give this statement without my parents present. Is that what you mean? Okay. (*Beat.*) You can call me Joey, yeah. That's fine. That's, like, what everyone calls me anyway. No one really calls me Joanna except, like, my grandma. (*Beat.*) So . . . Joey's good. (*Beat.*) My mom's still here, right? No, I'm fine. I don't need her to come in. I'm okay. I actually don't want to talk about all this stuff in front of her again right now. Or my dad. That was almost worse than the actual thing, you know, in a way . . . you know, having to tell my dad? I mean, not really. Obviously it wasn't *as bad* but . . . it's awkward now that I know he knows, 'cause he can probably, like, picture it. Which is like . . . I'm sorry, I actually don't feel that good. Could I have some water? Would that be okay? If it's too much trouble, that's totally fine, I just . . . No, I don't need my mom or anything. That's okay. (*Acknowledging the water, she takes a sip.*) Thanks. (*She takes a sip.*) I'm sure I'll feel better after I have a little of this. I just started feeling a little shaky. I'm okay. I'm so sorry. Um . . . okay . . . so, should I just start from the beginning? Okay.

(Lights up on JANE *standing stage left in a sweatshirt and jeans. She is in her kitchen talking to her mom.* JOEY *continues making her statement. The dialogue intertwines.)*

JANE. She just went to a party, like we all go to parties . . .

JOEY. Basically, the whole school was there.

JANE. Including me.

JOEY. My mom was comfortable with me going, because I was going with a few of my friends.

JANE. I *always* call you . . . but so does she. She always calls her mom . . .

JOEY. I told her I would call her when I got there and call her again when I left, and that I would take a cab home. That's our, like, usual deal when I want to go out. She calls it the Triple C: Call, Call, Cab.

JANE. What happened in that cab, Mom . . . (*Beat.*) She got in the cab with them because they are her friends. That's so crazy. They're our friends . . .

JOEY. Excuse me? Uh, yes. I would consider Luke a close friend, yes. Luke's mom and my mom have been friends for a long time because they were copresidents of the PTA in second grade. My mom thinks his mom's a little crazy, but our families are friends. I go to his house all the time.

JANE. I can't sleep . . . I barely slept last night. It's just . . . she wasn't supposed to be the only girl at his house. I was supposed to be there, and so was Anna. But Anna got grounded and you wouldn't let me go . . . If you had let me go she wouldn't have been alone. I just feel like some of this is on me . . . What?

JOEY. Because I wanted to. My parents were okay with it and I guess I thought it would be fun. It *was* fun at first, you know?

JANE. She said they were playing video games, they were dancing, they were. . . I *know* they were playing video games because she texted me her high score on Mario Kart while she was there . . .

JOEY. George brought the vodka. Uh, I'm not sure. I think his older brother got it for him.

JANE. I pregame, Mom. I'm sorry. I know you don't want to hear that, but . . . everyone pregames.

JOEY. I had some, yes.

JANE. Who told you she was sloppy drunk?

JOEY. I had two drinks . . . about two. And I know now that that was really stupid. I mean, obviously I wish I hadn't had any.

JANE. I don't understand . . . Okay . . . yeah, I saw them, too. But what is it that you think those pictures show, Mom? Have you seen *my* Instagram lately? She was just messing around. She wasn't sloppy drunk.

JOEY. I actually have, like, pretty little interest in drinking. I'm sure that sounds like a lie or, like, I'm trying to gloss over who I really am or whatever, but it's true . . . It's just sort of hard in certain moments to not do it. I know that's cliché but . . .

JANE. You talked to her about this? But you hate Linda. She sucks. You know she's just talking all this shit because her idiot douchebag son is involved. I mean, *where was she* when all this was going on? Out at dinner! So how would she even know? (*Beat.*) I don't care what the PTA moms think . . .

JOEY. Yes, I've been drunk before.

JANE. Yes, I know.

JOEY. And truth is, I wasn't drunk-drunk. I know what I feel like when I'm really drunk and I wasn't wasted. I just wouldn't be wasted after two or three, like, swigs of vodka. And, I'm not saying drinking is okay . . .

JANE. Yeah, I think in this particular situation, maybe that was a little stupid of her, Mom, yeah . . .

JOEY. It was stupid of me . . .

JANE. But you're not being realistic. I can't think of a single one of my friends who wouldn't have had a drink—

JOEY. I just can't believe this. I mean it's just . . . it was irresponsible of me to drink, I know, but I *was* trying to limit myself, you know. I was *trying* to be careful.

JANE. I feel like you're a different person right now. You've known Joey forever. She sleeps over here or I sleep over there, like, every week since we were nine! And you're acting like—you're acting like you don't believe her. I mean, you believe her, Mom, right? . . . Wait! . . . Are you kidding? What do you mean she exaggerates? What? When, when has she lied? (*Beat.*) That. Was. Eighth. Grade. So she told me she wasn't going to go to a party, and then she went, and I was upset because I felt left out. Whatever, Mom. I'm over it! You should get over it, too. Wow. This is really insane. You don't believe her . . . What the fuck? (*Beat.*) What, you're gonna ground me? Who cares! Do you think I give a crap, Mom? You know, it's really fucked because the funny thing is, we'd probably all be safer if we were all just grounded all the friggin' time, right?

JOEY. I wanted to party, I mean, I guess that's true. So . . . people think I'm a liar . . .

JANE. I can't believe you right now. You know what's so pathetic, Mom? No! I'm not going to stop! You always pride yourself on being this, like, big, like, feminist. You did that fundraiser downtown that time for women in India and wherever else, and you're always saying it's so messed up when people don't take women and girls seriously. And now *you're* not taking Joey seriously. You just called her a liar. You know, you said I could always come to you . . . but now I don't believe you . . . Because . . . What if that had been me? (*She starts to exit, but comes back.*)

JOEY. Stupid me, right? (*Sighs.*) I'm just so mad at myself for trusting them . . . and, like . . .

JANE. I heard you last night, Mom. (*Beat.*) You called her a slut 'cause of what happened. Yes, you did. You called her a "little slut" to Dad when you guys were in the kitchen. I heard you. (*Beat.*) If that had been me, Mom, and I had come to you . . . would you and Dad have called me a slut while making dinner when you thought I couldn't hear? Would the other moms be calling each other talking about what a slut I am, and what a liar I am, and what a sloppy, fucked-up drunk I was? (JANE *exits. Lights dim stage left.*)

JOEY. I just didn't think it would be like this. (*She drinks more water.*) Yeah, I'm fine. I'm sorry. (*Beat.*) Sorry? . . . Oh, uh, I don't know how much they had. I just don't remember. Um . . . I *do* know that we finished the bottle. I know that. Does that help? No, no one was high . . . I mean, does that even matter? I mean, does it matter if they smoke weed sometimes? Do I really have to answer that? Because they didn't have any that night so . . . No, I didn't feel like I needed to call my mom at that point. I had already called her when I got there. And honestly, things were normal. It was not the first time I drank with those guys. We drink together. I know we shouldn't, but we do. I wasn't uncomfortable or scared or anything. I was just hanging out with my friends . . . Right, he lives in the West Village . . . Sure. Tim Delaney, George Wright, and Luke Friedman . . . Uh, yes. Yes, I felt safe with them . . . Well, um, I guess I would say my relationship with them is pretty typical . . .

SCENE 2: GAME OF THRONES

SCENE: *Lights come up on* LEILA *and Danielle, stage left, sitting with their computers in* LEILA'S *room. They are eating a big bag of Twizzlers while scanning through Ask.fm.* JOEY *continues with her statement; the stories intertwine.*

LEILA. It's just so stereotypical to me, you know?

JOEY. They're my friends . . .

LEILA. They're her "friends."

JOEY. I've known them forever.

LEILA. Who she's known for, like, ever.

JOEY. We hang out every weekend, pretty much.

LEILA. They hang out every fucking weekend. Or better yet, she follows them around every weekend. You know it's true. Wherever George, Luke, and Tim go, she's there.

DANIELLE. I know.

JOEY. I know people maybe think I'm more than friends with these guys because we've, like, minimally made out before but—

DANIELLE. And what? She wants us to believe she's not secretly, or even obviously, into them? Please! Like she's *never* hooked up with any of them?

JOEY. I've never hooked up with any of them.

LEILA. Exactly. Whenever I ask George if they ever hooked up he's like, "Don't worry about it."

JOEY. We all know we're just friends, and we're cool like that.

DANIELLE. And it's so obvious what he means by that . . .

LEILA. Right. He means, "Yeah we've hooked up, but it was nothing. So don't let it get to you." And I don't. I actually don't totally care if they hooked up last year or whatever, but—

DANIELLE. Right.

LEILA. But Friday night—

DANIELLE. I know.

JOEY. Friday night—

LEILA. You don't do that.

JOEY. Was a pretty regular night, except I was the only girl.

LEILA. You don't do that shit with someone else's boyfriend.

DANIELLE. Oh.

LEILA. What?

DANIELLE. Is he really your boyfriend, though?

JOEY. Wait. (*Beat.*) I guess that's not totally the truth.

LEILA. What do you mean?

DANIELLE. Is he technically your boyfriend? I thought you guys were just hooking up.

JOEY. George was actually my first boyfriend.

LEILA. I don't get what you mean by that.

JOEY. He was my fourth-grade boyfriend, which is funny to think about. So, at one point we were more than just friends.

DANIELLE. I have just never heard anyone say he's your boyfriend, including you. And now all of a sudden he's, like, your boyfriend.

LEILA. We talk every day, we went to the movies once, we go to parties together—what do you think we are?

DANIELLE. Okay. Sorry. Maybe that's what you should ask on there. Make some comparison between you and her and see what he says.

JOEY. He was really different then. He carried a *Looney Tunes* lunch box to school. Sort of as a joke. And he had, like, Dennis the Menace hair. (*Beat.*)

LEILA. We haven't had sex.

JOEY. We held hands.

DANIELLE. Okay. Well, I didn't think—

JOEY. That was the extent of the physical contact.

LEILA. Do you think that's a big deal?

JOEY. It was such a big deal at the time, you know?

LEILA. I mean, we've hooked up a little bit but . . . only a little bit . . .

JOEY. I mean we all, like, whatever, with each other. It's nothing. It's just what you do.

DANIELLE. Okay. Well, what do you mean by a little bit? Like next to nothing?

LEILA. I don't know . . .

DANIELLE. You don't know what?

LEILA. Do you think that's why he's technically not my boyfriend?

DANIELLE. I don't know.

JOEY. Yes. Well, I don't know if she's his girlfriend, but George has been hanging out with this girl Leila lately.

DANIELLE. I think he's not technically your boyfriend because he's a junior and you're a freshman and, like, I don't know . . .

JOEY. She's a freshman.

LEILA. I fucking hate Joey Del Marco.

JOEY. She's actually pretty sweet and she's really pretty.

LEILA. I mean, I'm not ready to have sex with him, so she just makes herself available?

JOEY. I sort of feel bad for her because it seems like he's not really, totally into her.

DANIELLE. Yeah. That sucks.

JOEY. No, she wasn't at the party.

LEILA. Like, why weren't we invited to the party?

DANIELLE. Because we're freshman.

JOEY. There were no freshman allowed at the party.

LEILA. God, find your own guy, you stupid whore.

DANIELLE. I think she feels like those are her guys.

JOEY. But, anyway, most of the time George, Luke, and Tim just treated me like one of the guys. (*She takes a sip of water.*)

LEILA. Did she say that?

DANIELLE. No. Not to me but—

LEILA. So I'm just this freshman bitch to her who's taking over her territory?

DANIELLE. I don't know. And stop yelling at me. I'm just saying that's probably how she feels.

LEILA. Whatever. I don't understand why he won't call me or even just text me. I know he's around. What the FUCK?

JOEY. You know, I just don't understand how it got out of hand, you know? It's like, "What?"

DANIELLE. What are you gonna say?

LEILA. I'm gonna just, like, be there for him or whatever, and be, like, "Hey, I got your back."

16

DANIELLE. Why?

LEILA. What do you mean?

DANIELLE. Well, I just don't know why you'd say that exactly . . .

LEILA. Because I feel bad for him. Are you kidding me? This whole thing is a real shit show. This type of shit can ruin someone's whole life, and I feel bad for him. Because, you know, it's been his dream to go to Harvard like his dad. And his brother went there, too, and his grandfather and stuff, and this could 100 percent ruin that for him. He has got a 4.0 and his SAT scores were ridiculous and he's going to be scouted, or whatever you call it, for crew. It's just messed up . . .

JOEY. This whole thing is so messed up . . .

DANIELLE. Yeah, all of this is really messed up. But why are you getting his back?

JOEY. Back of a cab. They're telling everyone I hooked up with *all* of them in the back of that cab.

LEILA. Because I really like him and I know he didn't mean anything by it. They were wasted. Whatever—it happened. She's a slut, and she was all over his shit. Did you see those pictures? She was basically giving him a lap dance. What was he supposed to do?

DANIELLE. Leila, no matter what happened, right, no matter what actually happened, he still did it. And he's telling people that.

JOEY. They're telling everyone that . . . you know . . .

DANIELLE. You know what I'm saying? He's telling people he hooked up with her. He, like, admittedly messed around with someone else. And you're okay with that? (*Beat.*) You're still gonna hang out with this guy? I mean, what will your parents think? (*Beat.*)

LEILA. Do Joey and the Slut Squad talk shit about me at practice?

DANIELLE. No.

LEILA. Yeah, right.

DANIELLE. Dude, they don't. The only thing I've ever heard them say about you is that you're annoyingly pretty.

LEILA. See? They're out to put me in my place.

DANIELLE. I don't think they are but, okay. Honestly, Leila, I've never heard them say anything bad about you in the locker room or at practice. I would tell you. Why would I cover for them?

LEILA. Why is this happening to me?

JOEY. Why is this happening to me? I keep thinking that, you know? 'Cause we're not like this.

LEILA. I'm not even like this.

JOEY. This is not who we are. We're just not like this, you know?

LEILA. I'm not even into all this shit or whatever. You know I'm not . . .

JOEY. We're all like normal kids, you know?

LEILA. I mean, I don't want to be sitting here stressing about this shit.

DANIELLE. I know.

LEILA. I'd rather be in bed reading, like, I don't know, reading every *Game of Thrones* book all over again and—

DANIELLE. So why don't you? (LEILA *just gives her a look and goes back to her Twizzlers.*) Fine, so just keep hanging out with King Joffrey then!

LEILA. Stop. I am not Sansa!

DANIELLE. You are *so* Sansa . . . sorry.

LEILA. I'm Arya!

DANIELLE. No! You *want* to be Arya but—

(*Suddenly* LEILA *notices something on the computer. The latest Ask.fm post is projected on the screen.*)

LEILA. He answered one!

DANIELLE. Let me see. Move. (*They hover over the computer.*)

JOEY. I mean, you can see that, can't you? It's not who we are. (*She takes a sip.*)

LEILA. Someone was like, "What are you gonna say to Joey when you see her? Or are you never gonna talk to that nasty bitch again?" Okay, I love whoever asked that. So he wrote, "Yeah, we're definitely done with her. She's not a bitch, but we get it. She obviously regrets what she did Friday night, so she feels like she's gotta make shit up."

DANIELLE. Stupid.

LEILA. I'm gonna do it. I'm gonna write something. Hold on. (*She thinks.*) Okay. (*She types and Danielle reads over her shoulder. Her question is projected on the screen.*)

DANIELLE. "Do you think Joey was jealous of your relationship with Leila Zimmer and that's why she threw herself at you? Have you talked to Leila?"

LEILA. Good?

JOEY. I don't know, man . . .

DANIELLE. Yeah. It's good. Let's see what he says. (*They eat more Twizzlers in silence.*)

LEILA. Why is the sex in *Game of Thrones* always doggy style?

DANIELLE. No idea.

LEILA. Is that the only way they do it in Westeros? I mean—

DANIELLE. I know, right?

LEILA. I just . . . really like him.

DANIELLE. I know.

LEILA. "Winter is coming."

DANIELLE. Yup.

(*Lights dim on* DANIELLE *and* LEILA.)

JOEY. I just really liked them. That's the thing. Not like *that*, I swear to god. I just mean as friends. And yeah whatever. I'll just say it . . . I liked the attention. I'd be lying if I said I didn't. It's fun to have that attention, you know? I mean, all girls feel that way . . . and I mean any girl who says she doesn't is lying. I'm sorry. I love girls who say that, you know? Because they're lying. They're not above it, you know? They're just not. So . . . (*Beat.*) Do we really need to talk about that again? I just . . . Yes, CVS. Yeah. I had stopped there on the way to Luke's to get some deodorant. I was worried I smelled bad, okay? And then I was like, "Well, I haven't eaten all day really, so I need something to fill me up so I won't get sick if I drink" . . . So I got some Twizzlers and . . . No I'm okay. I'm just feeling really, like, frustrated with all this . . . Because it was just a stupid thing I did. I mean, haven't you ever done a stupid thing? I just don't get how this means that I . . . I mean, do you think they'll say that? Do you think that's what they're gonna say I was trying to do? . . . This is just so unbelievable!— Sorry. I'm sorry. I'm being really . . . rude to you, I feel like . . . No, I am. I'm sorry. I just sort of . . . hate . . . myself, but whatever. (*Building herself up a little . . .*) Let's just do this.

SCENE 3: JOEY BLOW ME

SCENE: *Lights come up stage left as* DOMINIQUE *and* JULIE *enter. They are roaming the aisles of the CVS, loitering in the cosmetics section. The condom aisle is projected on the screen.* DOMINIQUE *is texting.* JULIE, *looking at lip glosses, appears impatient.* JOEY *continues with her statement; the stories intertwine.*

JULIE. Let's just do this already.

DOMINIQUE. Hold on. (*She reads a text out loud.*) "Dominique ur magnifique." He's so the cutest, though, right? (*She continues to text.*)

JULIE. Dylan? Um, yes.

JOEY. Yes. I did it.

JULIE. Why don't you just ask him to do it?

DOMINIQUE. No. Are you stupid?

JOEY. And it was stupid, I guess. Another example of me being a stereotypical stupid girl that night.

DOMINIQUE. I'm not asking him to buy condoms.

JULIE. Why?

DOMINIQUE. Because then he'll think I want to have sex.

JOEY. I bought condoms and I brought them to Luke's. But that doesn't mean I wanted to have sex.

JULIE. But you do.

DOMINIQUE. Yeah, but I just don't want him to know that I want it, you know? It's too . . . odd. I just want to have some in my bag in case things start to happen. He, like, never has one. He just can't get it together, you know? So then this time we won't have to stop because *I'll* have one. And we won't go through that weird, unnecessarily awkward moment of, like, "Oh, let's just dry hump then . . . again."

JULIE. Okay, yeah. I get it.

DOMINIQUE. "Hey, can you get condoms for this weekend?" Don't you just think it will make me look weird?

20

JOEY. I get how it looks to everyone, you know?

JULIE. Yeah, it actually does sound like you're *Fifty Shades of Grey*-ing it!

DOMINIQUE. Yes! I know! (*They laugh. And then look around hoping no one from school is there.*) It's just way too Linda Lovelace for me.

JULIE. Way too Joey Del Marco for you. (*They laugh.*)

JOEY. It's not fair you know, because they don't know what I was thinking when I bought them. They all think they're mind readers, these people, and they're not.

JULIE. Whatever. Does your mom have any?

DOMINIQUE. What?

JULIE. What if you just searched through the bathroom drawers or bedside tables or something?

DOMINIQUE. Yeah. I'm not doing that, okay? I'm not using condoms my mom uses with the guys she meets on fucking eHarmony, okay?

JULIE. Okay!

JOEY. Okay. But I want to say that I didn't plan it.

JULIE. Come on. (JULIE *heads toward the condom section of the pharmacy.*)

JOEY. I got the candy and then I was like, "I'm gonna get them. It'll be funny." So I just went over to the condom section. (DOMINIQUE *and* JULIE *stand in front of the condom aisle.*)

DOMINIQUE. Oh my god.

JULIE. What?

DOMINIQUE. The pharmacist is definitely judging me right now. Why do they put them right here so you have to feel like a total dirty girl?

JULIE. I guarantee you she doesn't think you're a dirty girl.

DOMINIQUE. Why the fuck are there so many options?

JULIE. The different types do different shit. Ribbed are supposed to be good I think. (*Dominique is horrified. Julie, amused, points to a pack.*) Get those.

DOMINIQUE. Which ones?

JOEY. I got the ones I got not because I'm kinky or something but because it was a joke.

JULIE. The red and blue pack.

DOMINIQUE. (*She leans in to look.*) No! I don't want any kinky fire and ice shit. I'm not looking for fireworks, okay? I just want the basics.

JOEY. God . . .

JULIE. Oh my god, look!

DOMINIQUE. Shhh!

JULIE. Right there. Those are them. Flavored condoms. Oh my god, that's unbelievable. I mean, I would have killed to see the look on the cashier's face when she brought those up to the register.

DOMINIQUE. It probably turned him on.

JOEY. I didn't do it to turn them on. It wasn't like that. I mean, when you really think about it, how can flavored condoms be anything *but* a joke?

DOMINIQUE. Poor Joey.

JULIE. Joey Blow Me.

JOEY. Joey Blow Me. Not that clever, actually. Sort of fifth grade but . . . you know . . .

DOMINIQUE. Dude, stop.

JULIE. I'm just kidding, come on.

JOEY. But . . . you know . . . it still makes me feel like shit. It still sucks when your dad sees that shit online. (*Beat.*) And he looks at you like you're not you anymore . . . (*Beat.*) Yeah, I'm okay. Whatever. So, pretty much everyone thinks I bought them because I was planning on giving them all blow jobs and I wanted the blow jobs to taste like, I don't know, a rainbow of fruit flavors, I guess.

DOMINIQUE. (*She walks away from the section and motions for* JULIE *to follow her.*) Come here . . . come over here! My stomach is like flipping its shit . . . literally. I can't. I can't just stand there for, like, ten minutes in front of there and debate and discuss. Let's just talk about it over here.

JULIE. I don't think the ribs will hurt. I think they're small. They're just supposed to add, like, friction or something so it feels better? Maybe that's actually good? Just get those!

DOMINIQUE. Fine, fine . . . okay.

JULIE. What size?

DOMINIQUE. I have no idea.

JULIE. Dude, are you telling me you haven't seen his dick because, honestly, he's gonna put that in you and—

DOMINIQUE. No, no, no, no. I have, I have . . . obviously. But I don't, um, I don't really have anything to compare it to. I mean, how many penises do you think I've seen? I'm not a fucking whore.

JOEY. I mean people actually think I'm a fucking whore because of these condoms. Like I was actually going to blow three guys! Who would ever really do that? And it seems like you're saying that their opinion is, like, a big deal . . .

JULIE. Show me how big it is? (DOMINIQUE *reluctantly shows the size with her hands.*)

DOMINIQUE. Is that small? (JULIE *thinks for a second.*) Is it?

JULIE. I have no fucking idea! Fuck this, Dom. Just go to the nurse.

JOEY. If people could just understand where I was coming from, they would get it, maybe. I mean, maybe we could even call in the school nurse.

DOMINIQUE. Not possible! Not happening—never. I can't stand her face.

JOEY. Because that's how all of this started—with the condoms! Okay, because, okay—we were in health and she was leading a class about reproduction and, like, you know, everyone turned it into a sex talk.

DOMINIQUE. I don't want a sex lecture, or whatever.

JOEY. And Miss Garrison has this whole mission in health class. She doesn't want us to be afraid to ask questions.

DOMINIQUE. She acts like she's all cool, but she's not. She'll treat me like I'm making a bad decision. And she's always like, "no judgment," but that's bullshit.

JOEY. She lets us pass up anonymous questions at the end of class and the guys constantly try to throw her by asking something over-the-top sexual. But she never freaks out.

DOMINIQUE. Okay, I'm starting to freak out! What do I do?

JULIE. I don't know but . . . you're running out of time, babe, because I gotta go soon. I told Mari and Katie I'd meet them at six.

DOMINIQUE. (*Sighs.*) Fine . . . okay. What are you guys doing?

JULIE. Watching *Frozen*.

DOMINIQUE. I can't believe you're watching that again without me.

JULIE. So blow off Dylan and have a girls' night with us. You love girls' night!

DOMINIQUE. I can't . . . but I'm jealous.

JULIE. 'Cause girls' night kills it. Zero stress. I'm gonna get my Kristen Bell on, bitch. I'm gonna be all, like, (*sings*) "Do you wanna build a snowman . . ."

DOMINIQUE. (*Loving it, but trying to keep her quiet.*) Okay, okay, okay! Lovely . . . Hey, please promise you're not gonna tell them we were doing this today.

JULIE. Are you kidding? Dude, I would never do that. Come on. Just go over there, grab the first pack you see, and go to the checkout. I swear to god, no one gives a shit. Just do it.

JOEY. But these guys—Luke and Tim included—are idiots. They are really twelve years old. And they pass up a note that says, "Could you please explain the benefits of flavored condoms? I recently bought some grape-flavored ones and I'd be grateful for your advice."

DOMINIQUE. I wish I was one of those girls, you know? Someone who can just be, like, "Yup, I'm here to buy a pack of condoms because I'm going to have sex with my boyfriend, who I really love . . . "

JOEY. You would have loved it. Because she just says, "Some people use flavored condoms because it may make oral sex more pleasurable for the giver. They still successfully protect against pregnancy and STDs. The only warning I would issue is that sometimes novelty condoms can cause vaginal irritation."

DOMINIQUE. "And there's nothing wrong with that. I'm not some dumb little teenage whore. And I'll take the ribbed *and* the plain because I don't know what I like yet. And you can just deal with it, okay? Great."

JOEY. Great, right? I mean . . . the guys, Tim, Luke, Farid, Derek—I can name them all if you want—they went nuts. They were dying laughing.

DOMINIQUE. Why can't I do that? Like, it's no big deal. You know what I mean? You know those girls?

JULIE. Yeah, but those girls get themselves into Joey Del Marco situations.

JOEY. Does it make sense now—the condom situation? Tim, Luke, and George know it was a joke. I mean, we were reenacting Miss Garrison's whole speech! And now they're saying . . . I mean if they're saying that—

DOMINIQUE. What are you saying?

JULIE. I'm saying, Joey's all like, "I own my sexuality. Yeah I hook up, and I'm a badass, and I'm part of the Slut Squad"—and look where it got her. It landed her in the backseat of a cab with a group of guys who think she wanted it because, to be honest, she pretty much acts like she does, does she not?

DOMINIQUE. I don't know. It's like, we don't even know her really.

JULIE. I'm not talking shit, I'm just saying . . .

JOEY. There are pictures of me tasting the condoms online. I know that. And I hate that, okay? I'm, like, seriously upset about that. My parents . . . I mean, I can't even believe I did that. So it's stupid, okay? I'm aware. But everyone's acting like it's beyond fucked up. But . . . I'm not the only person with pictures like that. Is that really worse than a friend of mine who has a picture of herself online smoking a blunt? Or, like, blowing a banana?

JULIE. So, what? You're not talking to me now?

DOMINIQUE. What? No . . . no. I'm just surprised . . . that's all.

24

JOEY. I'm not surprised they took the pictures. Not totally shocking. But . . . *they* did it too. Did you see the pictures of *them*? You have those, right? So, am I not allowed to make stupid jokes, too?

DOMINIQUE. I mean, isn't she allowed to act like she wants it as much as she wants without, you know . . .

JULIE. I mean, can you imagine how fucking bad that was? No wonder she puked all over herself at Connor's.

DOMINIQUE. Dude, yes.

JOEY. I hate myself for doing it. Why did I do it? I ask myself that all the time. I don't even sleep because of that, you know. And I think, man, if I hadn't bought those things would it have even happened?

DOMINIQUE. I think they did it.

JOEY. Was that the one big trigger factor?

JULIE. So do I. But she *did* put herself in a fucked situation.

JOEY. I mean, do you think it was?

DOMINIQUE. Yeah, but I've put myself in fucked-up situations before.

JULIE. Oh, fuck yeah. Me too.

JOEY. And it's like, does that really invite what happened? You know? Buying the condoms made me seem into it—along with everything else about me, I guess. I understand how it looks. It's just not fair. It's bullshit.

JULIE. It's actually such bullshit 'cause every guy I know acts like he's all into sex and I've never heard of a group of girls holding him down and jerking him off, or sticking their fingers up some orifice. Except for in porn.

DOMINIQUE. (*Motivated.*) Okay, I'm getting them. I'm totally doin' it! The cashier can get over it.

JULIE. Dude, I think you're the one who needs to get over it.

DOMINIQUE. Fuck you.

JULIE. Nice. Hey, I'm getting this . . . what do you think? (*She holds up lip gloss and shows her lips.*)

DOMINIQUE. Do it. (DOMINIQUE *and* JULIE *exit. Lights dim stage left.*)

JOEY. So . . . we were messing around with the condoms and drinking at the same time. Yes, that's when the pictures were taken. I didn't know they uploaded them, no. But it's not like I would have been able to control that anyway . . . And I just wasn't thinking about . . . the impact of them . . . in that moment. I was drunk . . . (*Beat.*) Then I started getting texts from all my friends on the dance team saying they were on their way to the party. So we sort of cleaned up—got rid of the bottles and Luke took the opened condoms to his room because he didn't want his mom to find them in the trash. George stuffed the rest of them in his coat pocket and we left . . . No, we didn't even think of taking the subway. We just started looking for a cab. It was freezing. And I had bare legs. There was no way I was walking to the subway. We finally found a cab at, like, 9:30-ish. I remember the time because I texted my friend Jane telling her I was in the cab. You have that from my phone records, right? (*Beat.*) Yes, I'm on the dance team. I'm a junior, so it's my third year on the team. I think I could probably be captain next year . . . Yes. Does that matter? . . . Okay . . . Yes, I understand . . . Yes . . . The Slut Squad.

SCENE 4: SLUTTIN' IT UP

SCENE: *Lights up stage left as the* SLUT SQUAD *enters the locker room, now projected on the screen, after a Saturday night basketball game. They're not really talking to one another much. They start to get their stuff together.* JOEY'S *statement intertwines with the* SLUT SQUAD'S *dialogue.*

NATALIE. (*To* DANIELLE.) What are you doing?

DANIELLE. Wha—

NATALIE. Were you about to fucking come in here? (DANIELLE *stops dead in her tracks.*) Are freshmen allowed in here right now?

DANIELLE. No.

GRACE. So, stay out there. Right there. See that line? Don't cross that line until we're done. You wait in the doorway until we're done. Or did you forget that, Danielle?

NATALIE. I'm exhausted. (*She sighs.*) I cannot wait to get home . . . I'm gonna watch TV and do nothing. Did I tell you my dad is, like, obsessed with—(CHRISTINA *is making a show of shoving her stuff in her bag. She's clearly pissed at the others.*) Is there a problem or something, Christina?

CHRISTINA. Nope.

NATALIE. Really? (CHRISTINA *ignores her.*)

JOEY. Really? You think this is going to be an issue too? . . . How? (*Beat.*) Wow.

GRACE. Silent treatment. That's pretty ridiculous.

JOEY. It's just so ridiculous to me, you know? I don't know . . . this is . . . I'm just feeling sort of . . . I feel like every little aspect of my life is being ripped into with all of this . . . I know. I'm sorry that I keep, like . . . It's just, in any other scenario, you know.

CHRISTINA. Okay. You wanna know what's pissing me off?

NATALIE. Sure.

CHRISTINA. That was our worst performance of the season, mainly because you were fucking off. Every fucking time you do your new sequence, you're off.

NATALIE. What?

CHRISTINA. And it looks like shit.

NATALIE. Are you kidding me?

CHRISTINA. And no matter how many times Coach told you you weren't hitting the kick, no matter how many times she, like, drilled that with you, you still couldn't get it. What's your problem? It looked really fucking bad.

GRACE. Chrissy, she just learned it on Tuesday!

CHRISTINA. I don't give a fuck. She shouldn't even be doing it.

NATALIE. You. Are. Such. A. Bitch.

JOEY. When I started at Elliot, the dance team was already called the Slut Squad. I actually don't even know how long ago that started. So it's not like it was all our idea. It's just sort of a nickname; like in my cousin's school, there's a group of girls who call themselves the Dirty Dozen. It's just what the group of friends is known as. It's the same thing for us.

NATALIE. So I guess you think you should be doing it, right? You would have saved the day, right?

CHRISTINA. I think Joey should be doing it!

NATALIE. Well . . . in case you haven't heard . . . Joey was a little busy slutting herself out a couple of weeks ago so, unfortunately, she's no longer here with her perfect on-beat kicks.

GRACE. Jesus Nat—

NATALIE. So if you wanna be pissed at someone for tonight, Chrissy, be pissed at Joey.

JOEY. Are there requirements for being in the Slut Squad? . . . Well, yeah, you have to be on the dance team. That's pretty much it.

CHRISTINA. Well, that was pretty much the worst shit we've ever done.

GRACE. And it's not Natalie's fault, Christina. I mean, what the hell?

CHRISTINA. "What the hell?" Grace? We go out there, after all this shit with Joey, and the guys can't even keep the game *close* without Luke, and *she* dances like that—it's all fucking weak.

NATALIE. You're seriously overreacting.

CHRISTINA. Really? Well (*pointing toward* DANI-ELLE), that fucking freshman right there danced circles around you, so, hey if you're cool with that . . .

JOEY. It's sort of like a sorority . . . Is there hazing? No. Definitely not. I mean we're a little hard on the freshmen but it's just 'cause we want them to pay their dues, you know.

NATALIE. I'm telling you, Danielle, if you even smile a little . . .

JOEY. Stupid stuff like they have to wait until after we change to come in the locker room. And they can only speak when spoken to, which we honestly don't even really enforce because we like them. They're cute. And they have to go on Starbucks runs and dance in the back. It's not anything serious.

GRACE. Okay, so we fucked up a little. It was just the middle section. The opening was amazing.

CHRISTINA. Did you hear those kids from Leighton chanting in the left section?

NATALIE. Why are you doing this tonight?

GRACE. What were they saying?

CHRISTINA. I swear to god, I want to kill that dick Mark. You know he's Sam Beekman's cousin, right? I want to kill him and that whole crew of Leighton slut-bags he's always with at games.

NATALIE. Yeah, me too.

CHRISTINA. Well, why are you acting like you don't even care?

NATALIE. I *do* care but—

GRACE. Wait. What Mark guy?

NATALIE. He's that fat kid from Leighton. He's always in the stands with the red and gold Leighton sweatshirt and that fucking ski hat. I want to rip that fucking hat off his greasy fat head. He's an asshole because he's not on the team and it's the only way he can get girls.

GRACE. Okay. So what did he say?!

CHRISTINA. Unbelievable.

DANIELLE. "Leighton'll have you crying RAPE like a SLUT in the back of a cab—NO ESCAPE!" (*They all stare at her.*)

JOEY. It's not called the Slut Squad because we're actually, like, sluts . . . like in that way. No one is pressured to have sex . . . No. I mean, no . . . No one is, like, pressured into any type of sexual activity. I mean that would be so twisted . . . it's just not like that.

NATALIE. They were referencing Joey. Not us.

CHRISTINA. They're referencing the Slut Squad, are you kidding me?

JOEY. That's not even what "slut" really means to us.

GRACE. I can't believe Mr. Dowerly didn't say anything to them. They should have been kicked out for that.

CHRISTINA. They're saying we're a bunch of all-talk sluts who cry rape when things get tough.

NATALIE. Well, it's not true. When have I cried rape, Chris? Huh? (*Beat.*) When I hook up with someone, I take total responsibility for that, like anyone should . . . Unless it's like actually rape, okay? And don't get me wrong. I may not always be like, "Oh, awesome, I'm so totally proud of that choice!" But I don't pussy out and blame the guy. Neither does Grace, or you—or like any girl on this team. Not even the freshman—right, Dani?

DANIELLE. Yeah. (GRACE *shoots* DANIELLE *a look.*)

NATALIE. What?

DANIELLE. Nothing.

JOEY. When I think of what our idea of "slut" is on the team, and I know it sounds stupid now but . . . it's positive. We think it's wrong that guys can hook up with whoever they want and that's totally cool, but girls can't. It's an unfair double standard. So we're like, "Hey, if we act confident about sex and . . ."

NATALIE. (*To* DANIELLE.) We own our shit.

JOEY. "And we aren't afraid to be sexual. If all that makes us sluts, then I guess we're sluts." So, Slut Squad just means we're confident and, you know, sexy.

CHRISTINA. It's just that no one sees us that way anymore, Nat. Not since this. And it's humiliating. (*Beat.*)

GRACE. Have you talked to her?

CHRISTINA. Who, Joey?

GRACE. Yeah.

CHRISTINA. No. Have you?

GRACE. No.

NATALIE. I definitely haven't.

GRACE. She called me after she left Connor's, like five times.

NATALIE. Trying to get her story straight, I'm sure.

JOEY. It's only been after this that I've been called a slut in the way that means I'm really a dirty whore.

CHRISTINA. Yeah, well . . . whatever.

JOEY. I haven't talked to the girls on the team at all.

CHRISTINA. I don't want junior year to be like this now. With the fucking SATs coming up! Seriously. Fuck her, man.

JOEY. They just don't want to be a part of all of this, I'm sure.

NATALIE. And I mean, we're totally screwed for the rest of the season, right?

CHRISTINA. I just don't get why she's doing all this.

JOEY. No, none of them talked to me at the party. I mean, there's a good chance they just didn't even know what was going on. There were, like, forty people there, or something. But, no, we haven't talked since earlier that night.

GRACE. I feel bad.

JOEY. I sort of feel bad about that. Obviously. They're my friends so . . . I'm pretty sure that means they don't believe me . . . which I mean . . .

CHRISTINA. Honestly, that's, like, the only thing I have to say to her, Grace: Why. Are. You. Doing. This?

NATALIE. For the attention.

GRACE. She doesn't need to do that for attention.

NATALIE. Why are you defending her, Grace?

GRACE. I'm not!

CHRISTINA. Do you really think they raped her, Grace? Rape?

GRACE. I don't know.

NATALIE. Come on.

GRACE. Those guys can be like . . . (*Trying to figure out how to say it.*) . . . George . . . I mean . . . I . . .

NATALIE. Your ex-boyfriend is a rapist. That's what you're saying?

GRACE. No, Nat . . .

CHRISTINA. I've known Joey since kindergarten. She loses control sometimes. She's done weird shit before. That night I think she got back to her house with Jane, and her parents were there, and she just started lying, you know?

NATALIE. Yeah.

JOEY. So you think the fact that my dance team is called the Slut Squad is going to make people think that I must be an actual slut—

CHRISTINA. And she's really screwed over the whole school.

JOEY. They'll say I'm "admittedly promiscuous"? I hate the word promiscuous. (*Beat.*) So that implies what? That I couldn't have been . . . you know . . . raped, then? That cancels out the possibility of rape to people? (*Beat.*) That's . . . crazy.

NATALIE. So what should we do?

JOEY. So what should I do?

CHRISTINA. Get our shit together 'cause another night like this can't happen. And don't talk about Joey. No more online shit either. I don't wanna be associated with her.

NATALIE. Okay.

CHRISTINA. And, Nat, you seriously gotta work on that sequence or give it away. 'Cause it's just pulling us down even more. For real.

NATALIE. Fine. (*Her phone rings.*) Hold on. (NATALIE *answers her phone.*) Hi Mom . . . Yeah, it was okay . . . No, it's just a bad night. We lost. No, yeah, I'm good . . . Yeah, tell Dad to wait for me. Uh—Pepperoni? Okay, I'm coming home now. Love you. (*She hangs up.*) You'll work on it with me Monday? (CHRISTINA *nods. They hug goodbye. Say "Love ya's."* NATALIE *exits.*)

CHRISTINA. Bye Gracie. (*To* DANIELLE.) You did a good job, tonight, you know? (DANIELLE *nods.* CHRISTINA *exits.*)

JOEY. You know, I feel like everything I've ever done is so stupid.

GRACE. (*To* DANIELLE.) You thinking about Silas?

DANIELLE. No.

GRACE. You never told them about that, I guess, right?

DANIELLE. No.

GRACE. Hey, he's an idiot.

DANIELLE. Yeah.

GRACE. You know, George once followed me into the bathroom and locked the door and wouldn't let me out until I gave him a hand job. True story. I didn't tell anyone. We ended up going out for, like, five months . . .

JOEY. All I want to do is, like . . . cry . . . No. Actually even better. Go back in time. I wish I could go back in time. Someone needs to invent a time machine now.

GRACE. (*Starts to leave.*) You can go in now. Hey, I mean, you know Christina and Natalie aren't really like that, obviously. They're just worried about the team, you know? (DANIELLE *nods and* GRACE *heads for the door.*)

DANIELLE. (*She stops* GRACE, *obviously uncomfortable.*) Wait. Grace—I wanted to tell you that . . . um . . . I'm quitting the team. I just . . . I don't know . . . my schedule is just too nuts and I really can't keep up anymore, so I'm going to tell Coach that I—

GRACE. You can't. Sorry. There's too much going on right now and we really need you. Sorry. You can't quit, okay? (DANIELLE *just stares at* GRACE *as she leaves.*) Hey, good job, tonight! See you Monday. (DANIELLE *just stands there.*)

JOEY. This is just getting worse. (DANIELLE *exits. Lights dim stage left.*) So, that's the deal with the Slut Squad . . . Oh, sure. Of course. No problem. I'm totally fine, yeah . . . No, I'm good. Okay . . . (JOEY *watches the Assistant District Attorney leave the room. She is alone for a moment . . . she breathes, puts her head on the table. She hears the door open . . . her visitor catches her by surprise.*) Hey Dad . . . I'm good . . . Yeah, she just stepped out for a second to use the bathroom . . . Yeah, I'm just tired. What's Mom doing? . . . Okay, good . . . It's going okay, I think, but I don't really know . . . It's just—everyone pretty much hates me, Dad, and I don't know . . . I'm really sorry about all of this, Dad . . . I know . . . (*She smiles a little—tries to prove she's "okay."*) I know . . . Yeah, I'm fine . . . You should go . . . 'Cause I can hear her coming back . . . Okay—okay . . . just go, okay? . . . I know . . . I love you too . . . Yeah, I'm gonna be fine . . . Love you. (JOEY *watches her dad leave. The Assistant District Attorney is back.*) Hi. Yeah, my dad just popped his head in to say "hi." They're just worried, you know . . . but I'm okay. So, okay . . . So, I found a cab after about five minutes . . . On 8th Avenue. Right on the corner of 8th and Horatio, and we all got in the backseat. (JOEY *drinks her water and composes herself.*) I remember the driver was black—but, um, African. Not African American, but actually he was from Africa, I think. I'm sorry. I sound like such a jerk, right? I'm sorry. He had an African name, I know that. Like . . . Batuba, or something, but it wasn't Batuba. I don't really remember specifically what he looked like. He was very dark skinned and had a shaved head and no facial hair. Maybe he was, like, fortyish. Do you think there's any way to track him down? I mean, if I saw him I might recognize him. Don't they have to submit a log or something? Is it possible to trace the starting and ending points of our trip or whatever, or. . . Okay, yeah . . . He had an accent, I know that, and he was playing music pretty loud.

SCENE 5: BROS BEFORE HOS

SCENE: *Lights come up stage left on* ANNA *in her bedroom. Loud music is playing. She is wearing pajamas and reading something on her computer. Her brother Tim knocks on her door.* ANNA *doesn't hear him at first.* JOEY *continues with her statement; the stories intertwine.*

JOEY. And I remember Tim asked him to turn it down a little.

ANNA. (*She looks up and sees Tim.*) What?

JOEY. And the guy completely ignored him.

ANNA. (*Turns down the music.*) What's up? . . . Okay, well it's down now so . . .

JOEY. Yes, so it was Tim, Luke, me, then George. And, sort of, in order for us all to fit comfortably . . .

ANNA. What?

JOEY. I just sort of slung my leg over George's.

ANNA. Nothing.

JOEY. It was nothing. I mean my dress was still covering me, you know?

ANNA. Just, you know looking at Facebook and stuff. (*Beat.*) Okay. Hey—can you shut the door? (*She heads back to her computer and sees that he hasn't left.*) What? . . .

JOEY. What were we doing?

ANNA. Why? What's she doing? . . .

JOEY. Just hanging out, you know, and—

ANNA. Is she yelling at Dad or just crying again?

JOEY. We were sort of talking, but the music was pretty loud.

ANNA. Well . . . what do you want her to do? . . . This is all like . . . bad, Tim, and . . .

JOEY. It wasn't bad right away.

ANNA. She loves you . . . so . . . it's just . . . bad.

JOEY. I don't even know how it all happened.

ANNA. How am I looking at you? . . . No, I'm not . . . I haven't at all! . . . I have not. The past three weeks, all I do is go to school, and pick up Thea, come home and you guys are always huddled in the kitchen or somewhere, and I'm not a part of any of this. Then come in and shut the door then—but I haven't been looking at you like anything! . . . No . . . I'm just . . . Tim, you know . . . you're my brother (*She has a hard time saying this.*) . . . and I'm really worried about you . . . (*She tries to compose herself.*)

JOEY. Yeah, I'm okay. It's just—I hate this . . . aspect of it the most. I think about it all the time, but saying it out loud . . .

ANNA. I mean . . . did you do it? . . . Yes, I know what you said! I *do* believe you. I mean, you're like my best—(*Beat.*) But, if you didn't do anything, then why were you fucking arrested, and you're on academic probation, and—

JOEY. I sort of don't understand how I should say all of this? I should say all the details right?

ANNA. So tell me, then . . . just tell me what happened, because . . . Mom and Dad know the details, and the lawyers, but I don't know anything, and I'm at school all day hearing all this stuff, and we haven't talked about it, and. . . Okay . . . Okay, I know. . . . I'm sorry. . . . So—tell me.

JOEY. We were kind of dancing in the back, and George was sort of keeping the beat on my leg, you know, sort of like, I know this sounds weird, but playing drums on my leg.

ANNA. Yes, I know how Joey gets when she's drunk.

JOEY. And then George and I started to, like . . . make out for a second, but it was only for a second, and then he started to put his hand up my leg.

ANNA. But, I also know how *you guys* get when you're drunk.

JOEY. I just sort of slapped it away, like, in a friendly way, but then he did it again but . . . this time his hand actually went up my dress and sort of grazed my crotch. (*Beat.*) I guess I started to get nervous at that point. My heart started really beating, and I remember tightening up and kind of clamping down on his hand with my hand. (*Beat.*) I looked at him and he was looking sort of past me at Luke with this face on. I mean, I don't know how to describe the face, but, sort of like "Hey, man, look what *I'm* doing." So I said, "George, come on, stop. Just wait until we get to Connor's." . . . I'm not sure I said "stop," exactly, but I mean it was clear that I wanted him to stop because I was trying to pull my leg down off his, you know? And I was trying to push his hand off me, but he was grabbing my skin, sort of clawing it a little. (*Beat.*) I don't know. I don't know if I actually would have done anything with him at Connor's. I was just saying that so he would stop doing the stuff right there in the cab. I was trying to offer something up, you know? It seemed like a good idea at the time . . . (*She takes a sip of water.*)

ANNA. Nothing . . . Sorry, nothing . . . I'm just picturing her you know . . . Sorry, so then what?

JOEY. So then, next thing I know, Luke is grabbing my other leg . . . Pulling my leg to the side, so my, um, legs would be more open and George—then George kind of moved his body so *his* leg was on top of my leg, sort of pinning me down. It was pretty much impossible for me to move because their bodies were pressing my arms against the back of the seat—like this. So my arms are like this, and George starts pulling at my dress, pulling it up farther. (*She drinks water.*) Like, how much detail do you need?

ANNA. I hate thinking of her struggling. George and Luke are so much bigger than her. I would have been beside myself—hysterical, being, like, pinned down by the two of them. I would have been screaming like a psycho. I don't get them.

JOEY. Then George all of a sudden really aggressively pulls my underwear to the side and jammed two of his fingers inside me. (*Beat.*)

ANNA. That's disgusting. (*Beat.*) So, what did you do? . . . What did you do when they started doing that?

JOEY. I was crying at this point, but I didn't scream. I just couldn't. I couldn't make a scream come out. It felt like I was choking.

ANNA. And the driver didn't notice anything?

JOEY. The music was pretty loud, like I said, so the driver, I guess, just couldn't hear anything. I remember just staring so hard into the rearview mirror, wondering if he would catch my eye. I was horrified at the thought. I was so embarrassed. I mean, I was disgusting. My vagina was pretty exposed, and I kept thinking if this guy turns around to check on us and sees me like this, we're going to get in an accident.

ANNA. Why didn't you stop the cab?

JOEY. George had his fingers in me . . . Two . . . Yes, I'm sure . . . Because I saw them! (*Beat.*) Okay, so, and he was sort of—uh, um—moving them in and out as hard as he could and as fast as he could. Kind of in a stabbing motion. And he was really putting his whole body into it, and I was . . . I was clenching pretty hard, does that make sense? I was squeezing everything, trying to sort of close myself up . . . and I think that made it hurt even more. And I'm crying. And the whole time Luke is making fun of George because I'm . . . you know . . . you know . . . because I'm not coming. Because I'm not having an orgasm. He was laughing and saying, like, "Dude, do you even know what the fuck you're doing? You're giving the poor girl fucking pussy burn. You make girls cry you're so bad at that shit." That type of stuff, and George was like, "Fuck you—it's not me—" And then he said . . . he said, "Her pussy's as dry as a fucking desert." (*Beat.*) He finally pulled his fingers out. Luke was laughing and he was bragging how he was going to show George how it was done. Then he put two of his fingers in his mouth. And I just really started to go crazy because I knew what was coming and . . . that's when George said, "I feel like we're fucking wrestling an alligator or some shit."

ANNA. Did he seriously say that?

JOEY. (*Visibly shaken.*) I need a second, okay? (*She tries to breathe.*) So George says the alligator thing and then Luke laughs—and then he stuck his wet fingers in my vagina. (*She has a hard time with this next sentence.*) He told me he wet his fingers because I was so dry. (*Beat.*) Then he did the same thing as George except he was trying to show off. I was hysterically crying, and he kept saying things like, "Come on JoJo—you know you wanna come—you know you're wet now." And then he seemed to get tired or, I don't know, annoyed with me, and he said, "Wow—guess you're all talk, huh, Joey?" And he and George laughed. Luke pulled his fingers out of me and wiped them on George's shirt. And then they let go of me. (*Beat.*)

ANNA. I hate them.

JOEY. I hate them whenever I think about it.

ANNA. That is the most fucked up thing I've ever heard. I don't understand. She said, "No," right?

JOEY. Yes, during the whole thing I kept saying, "Come on you guys. Don't. No. No, I don't want to do this."

ANNA. So what were *you* doing?

JOEY. Tim was just looking out the window.

ANNA. Why didn't you do anything? . . . You sat there, Tim. You didn't stop the cab. You didn't text anyone. You didn't even say anything to them! . . . Um, like, "What the hell are you guys doing? Stop." . . . But you were a part of it! You were right there while two of your best friends were doing crazy shit to a girl you've known your whole life, and she clearly wasn't into it.

JOEY. I really don't want him to get in trouble for this. He's a good guy and he works really hard and stuff. And he's one of my really good friends. I think he just probably didn't know what to do and that's not his fault. He's the twin brother of one of my best friends, you know? Anna. I haven't talked to her since this.

ANNA. But, I mean, you looked at your phone and stared out the fucking window. Why? . . . Maybe you were drunker than you thought?

JOEY. I don't feel very well.

ANNA. Because you *know* her! She's one of my best friends. She's gone camping with us, Tim.

JOEY. I'm sorry. How much longer do you think we'll be?

ANNA. You're right, I really don't get it. . . . Were you afraid they were going to hurt you or something? I mean, I know what they're like when they're drunk. Like that time in Brooklyn when Luke took that rock from in front of the church on Clinton Street and then smashed the window of that car. That was fucking crazy. He was out of control. Did you think they would—

JOEY. No . . . I'm okay—I'm fine to keep going . . .

ANNA. Okay! So then tell me. Because I know you better than anyone and you're not like this. (*Quieting her voice so the rest of the family doesn't hear.*) And I keep thinking about Thea, Tim, and how we'd literally kill anyone who ever did anything close to that to her. I mean picture her. Not knowing what to do and feeling scared and trapped. And that's how Joey felt and . . . you just didn't help her. And you're an awesome guy. And you may have just fucked your whole life. And that's why this whole thing is a fucking nightmare, or something, because you are NOT that guy.

JOEY. The last thing I remember seeing before it started was Columbus Circle mall.

ANNA. I know it happened fast.

JOEY. When they were done we were at 78th and Lex. I saw the street sign. No—

ANNA. No, I won't—tell me.

JOEY. I didn't get out. I should have, I guess. But I didn't know what to do. My underwear was ripped and I was sore. I just stared at the taxi TV. (*Beat.*) They tried to talk to me, you know? They teased me for ignoring them. Luke put his arm around me and said, "Give me a hug. You're, like, the most down girl ever." . . . No, Tim didn't join the conversation. He was still just looking out the window.

ANNA. (*She stares at him. The answer surprises her.*) You didn't want to be a pussy. (*Beat.*)

JOEY. The cab pulled up to Connor's building. I gave ten bucks.

ANNA. That's totally fucked. And I believe you, Tim. And I understand and I love you a lot, okay? (*Beat.*) But you gotta know that's totally fucked. "Guys don't do that to other guys." (*Beat.*)

JOEY. I locked myself in the bathroom when I got there. And I threw up everywhere.

ANNA. (*Trying to understand her brother.*) Because, so what if they called you a pussy? What would have happened? Would you have lost them as friends, do you think? Would you have died? (*Beat.*) So then don't be a pussy, Tim.

JOEY. Jane helped me. I told her what happened and she gave me her underwear. We called my mom and then we got in a cab. We got to my house at 10:45-ish.

ANNA. Why would the lawyers say that?

JOEY. I told my parents. My mom put my underwear in a ziplock baggie. I think she thought there was "evidence" on them but . . . you know. They were really good about it. My dad cried, which really made me cry.

ANNA. But that stuff doesn't matter 'cause you know they did it.

JOEY. I know they're disappointed, you know?

ANNA. Yes, more than anything, obviously, I want what's gonna be best for *you.* I just don't understand how that's right, though. (ANNA *hears her mom call to her; she takes a breath.*)

ANNA. Yeah, Mom? . . . He's right here . . . Okay . . . We're coming. (*She looks at him. They share an "our mom is annoying and losing it" look.*) I hate our family like this . . . (*Beat.*) Go . . . Yeah, I'm okay. I'm just realizing I'm probably never going to talk to Joey again, right? (ANNA *exits. Lights dim stage left.*)

JOEY. Ten to fifteen minutes. Everything happened in only, like, ten to fifteen minutes. That's it. That's all it took for my life to . . . just . . . implode. (*Beat.*) And now I'm Slutty Girl who shouldn't have gotten drunk, and shouldn't have been there, and shouldn't have done all the things that everyone says I shouldn't have done. But how is it all about everything *I* shouldn't have done? So now I'm that girl.

SCENE 6: RAPE GIRLS

SCENE: *Lights come up stage left on Starbucks.* SYLVIE *enters. She has a Starbucks cup and pastry bag. She settles herself in at a table, takes off her coat, and looks around. She's meeting someone.* JOEY *continues with her statement; the stories intertwine.*

JOEY. And I don't want to be.

SYLVIE. Thanks for meeting me here. I hope this isn't too random or, like, weird . . . Good . . . um, do you wanna get something? I got hot chocolate while I was waiting. Get in line if you want. Oh, okay . . . You sure?

JOEY. Sure . . . I mean, I *thought* I knew the point of doing all this, sure. But the thing is actually *doing* all this . . . is what makes me like that girl. The minute I went with my parents and Jane to the precinct that night; and the minute I filed the report; the minute they got arrested—I became her.

SYLVIE. I love your scarf. It looks really good on . . . did you make it? It looks homemade . . . Oh . . . Right . . . Yeah I love that place . . . You're welcome. So, when was the last time you saw Caroline? I honestly haven't seen her since that party she had. Which is crazy 'cause that was like freshman year, right? . . . Yeah . . . I mean we Facebook each other but . . . Yeah, it's weird because I met so many people at that party . . . I know! It was, like, the craziest party ever. And it's just funny because I'm better friends with some of the most random people I met there than I am with Caroline now . . . Yeah, we did, but then she left. She goes to, yeah, Bronx Science, yeah. I guess she likes it. I don't know.

JOEY. I know . . . I know, I understand . . . I know you are . . . And I really appreciate everything you guys are doing so much . . .

SYLVIE. So . . .

JOEY. So, I'm sorry if it ends up that I was just wasting all your time . . .

SYLVIE. How is everything going?

JOEY. Because . . . how do you think this is all going?

SYLVIE. I'm sorry. Am I an asshole for asking that? I just . . . I don't know what I should or shouldn't say and . . . (*She laughs awkwardly.*) Right, sure. Sorry, I'm just—

JOEY. No, I'm just asking. Because, I mean, do you really think anything will come of this? . . . Well, what does a really good chance mean? . . . But what do we have? . . . besides my ripped underwear, which you said doesn't exactly prove assault. It's basically what they say versus what I say, right? (*Beat.*)

SYLVIE. I saw what people were saying about you online and stuff and I . . .

JOEY. I lose then. I can see it happening.

SYLVIE. I just couldn't . . . it was really fucked up. People are, like, really twisted, huh?

JOEY. I lose!

SYLVIE. It's like you never think people will actually say such stupid shit, right?

JOEY. BECAUSE I'M A SLUT!

SYLVIE. I mean, you hear about it in the news.

JOEY. Haven't you heard? I mean, you didn't know that?

SYLVIE. But when you really see it and people you sorta know are writing it . . .

JOEY. I'm a whore.

SYLVIE. It's surreal. I'm sorry you've had to go through that. I'm just— really sorry. Seriously.

JOEY. But seriously, think of everything we just talked about! (*Beat.*) Who would you believe? Really. Be honest. I wouldn't even believe me, probably? So I'm a slut *and* a liar to everyone, you know? And it's like it doesn't matter what really happened, because no one will ever really know.

SYLVIE. It fucking sucks.

JOEY. And I'm just tired. And I don't want to do this! I'm tired of explaining everything. I know I probably should have to. I guess that's only fair. But I'm tired of it and I'm just . . . totally humiliated. And I . . . don't like my life like this! . . . I don't want it like this. I don't want my parents missing work to sit in a waiting room or to stay home with me because they're afraid I'm fucking suicidal or something. (*Beat.*) No . . . I'm not. I shouldn't have even said that. I'm sorry. I'm not at all. I'm . . . I'm . . . I'm just aware that I'm making their life awful and . . . everything they, you know, like, wanted for me . . .

SYLVIE. Have you been getting ready for the SATs? . . . I have this tutor. She's pretty good. I got the book, whatever. I just suck at standardized tests, you know? So bad news for me, huh? Bye bye Harvard, I guess, right? (*Awkwardly laughs.*) Exactly. I know. Do you have a list yet? . . . A college list? . . . My parents made me make one . . . Wesleyan? Really? . . . That's a really good school. That's awesome . . . Yeah . . . Well, if you apply early and get in, you don't need to worry about a list, right?

JOEY. I ruined all that by putting myself in the situation I did. (*Beat.*) And then coming forward . . . just made it all worse, actually.

SYLVIE. Actually . . . my brother goes to my dream college. I love the campus. I don't know, after being in the city my whole life, there's just something about a campus with Gothic buildings and trees and hills and nature and quiet—sounds so good to me. Sort of old school, you know? I just fell in love with it. Honestly, I don't even know if I'll be able to get in, that's the thing.

JOEY. I just don't know about this anymore! I mean, what do—what do you think will happen? . . . Seriously.

SYLVIE. Seriously, are you sure you don't want anything? Want a piece of my cookie?

JOEY. But, do you think Tim would do that? . . . Then why hasn't he done that yet? What's their thinking?

SYLVIE. You're probably thinking, "Why did this, like, random girl wanna hang out out of nowhere?"

JOEY. (*Shocked.*) Is it really possible that the charges will be dropped?

SYLVIE. Can I ask you a question?

JOEY. I keep asking myself . . .

SYLVIE. What made you say something? (*Beat.*) I mean, how did you, like, knowing that you were going to get so much shit coming at you.

JOEY. Over and over again—

SYLVIE. How did you do it?

JOEY. "Why did I do this?" If I hadn't reported it . . . it would be old news . . . I swear to god . . . it would have already been old news by now. It would have been this crazy, shitty thing that happened. No, no, actually, you know what? No one probably would have known but the guys and me because the only reason they started saying all that shit was because I *reacted* . . . I got all upset, and I left the party, and I wouldn't talk to them. So they went into major defense mode.

SYLVIE. Because I think it's really . . . I don't know . . . I think it's really brave. I don't know how you did it. I mean, you don't have to tell me . . . we don't even really know each other . . . I just—

JOEY. I just totally fucked myself.

SYLVIE. I don't know.

JOEY. No, I don't want them to come in right now. It's going to get them all upset and I just don't want to do that to them . . . (*Beat.*) I'm sorry, I'm really sorry. Obviously, I'm having some kind of panic thing. I'm really sorry. (*She tries to breathe.*) So, okay, if the charges don't get dropped, what will the story be?

SYLVIE. So, I went to visit my brother at school last year . . . He's a junior now. We're four years apart. I actually stayed there on campus with him and everything. Went to a really cool class on mid-twentieth century French film—totally what I'm into, and I was just really excited to be there. I slept right on the floor next to his bed. And we went to the local pizza place—just so good . . .

JOEY. Is that good? So, what would that scenario look like? . . . Okay, but if they cop a plea will the assault still be on their record? . . . What does it depend on? . . . So . . . What then, they'll . . . at the very, very least . . . (*Beat.*) Interesting. It will *always* be on *my* record . . . No, I mean . . . not technically but . . . in the minds of everyone that knows about this . . . I'll always be the girl from high school who claimed she was raped.

SYLVIE. The second night I was there, I was raped. (*Beat.*) Sorry to just throw that out there like that, but . . . I wanted you to know why I wanted to . . . to talk to you. I don't even use that word that much. 'Cause it's weird and even though that's what it was—and it was—I don't know . . . I just don't wanna be a rape girl, you know?

JOEY. I'm sorry.

SYLVIE. I mean, of course you know—duh. So I rarely use the word . . . I don't ever talk about it either . . . you know, to regular people.

JOEY. And they'll be regular people, back to partying every weekend . . . they'll be these poor wronged guys, back on the basketball team, back on the road to the Harvard dorms, right?

SYLVIE. My brother took me to a party at the dorm next to his. I honestly don't think I've ever been as excited and nervous and totally, like, pathetically insecure as I was that night. College parties are fucking ridiculous, okay. And my brother was like, "Please be fucking careful. I don't want to get in trouble because you're underage, and at this party, and drinking, and whatever. Just don't leave without me and don't leave the dorm. I don't want campus security seeing you. I'll be totally fucked if they catch you stumbling across campus, okay?" And that scared the shit out of me, but I was, like, "Yeah of course." (SYLVIE *sips and eats—as does* JOEY.)

JOEY. Next year I'm going to officially transfer to that school up near my grandparents upstate. It's a good school. But I'll be a senior, so I won't really have a chance to settle down there and fit in or whatever.

SYLVIE. I don't think I've ever tried so hard to fit in in my life. And the whole time I was like, "Damn it. I'm not wearing the right thing; I'm not saying the right shit; I look like I'm frigging thirteen. There's no way any of these guys will ever go for me. I'm such a loser." You know? It was just crazy. I remember this girl Jessica that was there, and I wanted to be her so bad. She was like the epitome of New England college girl hot you know? I could just tell she was, like, a Russian Lit major, or whatever, and she looked perfect smoking a joint and the guys were literally all over her. Anyway . . .

JOEY. So, in a way, we may all get the same punishment, the guys and me, for being bad . . .

SYLVIE. So I was bad. I smoked. I'd never smoked weed before and it just really fucked me up. I think maybe it was laced with something, because I was out of it. But I don't know, because I had never done it so I don't have anything to compare it to. But I was like funny-mirror-in-a-fun-house out of it, you know?

JOEY. I know . . .

SYLVIE. I knew I had to stay in the building, so I made my way down the hall. I wanted to get it together, you know? I found this room with a poster of Dwight from *The Office* on the door. I went in. No one was in it and it had a bathroom. I tried to make myself throw up, but it didn't work. I don't know if that would have made a difference.

JOEY. So, you know, is any of this really making a difference?

SYLVIE. Because I think the weed fucked me up. I had only had one drink.

JOEY. I mean, I went to my friend's house and had two drinks and—

SYLVIE. So then I splashed water on my face and just tried to get it together.

JOEY. Everything fell apart! And I'm, like, I feel like I'm at the bottom of this fucking pit—

SYLVIE. When I came out of the bathroom—

JOEY. And I can't get out of it at all.

SYLVIE. This kid was in the room. We started talking about, like, nothing, and then out of nowhere he just grabbed me and literally threw me on the bed. (*Beat.*) He didn't hit me or anything. Nothing like that. (*Beat.*) I know I said, "Stop." I didn't say "No." He leaned his whole upper body on my head and covered my mouth with his forearm. He smelled like beer. I mean, he didn't even look at me. (*Beat.* SYLVIE *sips to hide tears.*) And he . . . you know . . . (*Beat.*) I had never had sex before. And it was worse than I ever thought it would be, and I was sort of always scared of sex.

JOEY. I remember what I told you, yes!

SYLVIE. When he left the room, I got up and ran to the bathroom. I washed the shit out of my body and my mouth and everything.

JOEY. I told you I was angry.

SYLVIE. And it's weird because not even for a second did I think: DNA— don't wash yourself! I mean, I'd seen *SVU* like a thousand times, but I didn't even think about evidence, you know? I just wanted it off me, you know. (*She looks around to make sure no one is really listening.*) I remember feeling so glad that he didn't, you know, come in me, but I was freaked for weeks about STDs and getting pregnant. I kept examining myself for herpes or genital warts. I stayed up every night WebMD'ing myself to death.

JOEY. I was angry because . . . they . . . took something from me—

SYLVIE. So, anyway, I put my clothes on and walked out of the room and the party was fully going on.

JOEY. And they humiliated me and . . . made me feel like . . . a piece of shit! Like I was an idiot piece of trash.

SYLVIE. I mean, I knew I wasn't going to tell immediately. I played the whole thing out in my head.

JOEY. I told you that they were my friends . . . And that I felt they had betrayed me, and just completely violated me.

SYLVIE. Everyone would know—my brother, that Jessica girl—the school would know. They would never admit a girl who was, you know . . . you know, on their campus—an underaged girl who shouldn't have even been there. I was worried my brother would get in trouble and kicked out. And everyone at home would know. Other colleges. It would be on my record, or whatever. There was no way I could do it.

JOEY. And I'm pissed—

SYLVIE. That Jessica girl came up to me and told me my brother had gone to get more beer. She was just really sweet to me.

JOEY. Because they seemed to think they could do that to me. Like it was no big deal to them. (*Beat.*)

SYLVIE. The guy's name is Jeff. He graduated at the end of last year.

JOEY. And that's . . .

SYLVIE. I didn't tell my parents.

JOEY. Wrong. And I know it's wrong with, like, every little part of me.

SYLVIE. My brother and I don't talk as much now. I feel like he knows something. I did tell one of my friends and she didn't know what to say.

JOEY. I told you that I knew I had made some bad decisions and that I had put myself in not the best situation. But that, "so what?" I told you I had said, "No," and that I had begged them to stop. And they didn't and . . . no matter what I did. They were wrong. And you told me this would be hard and—and I said I didn't care—because—

SYLVIE. I think what you did was really . . . amazing.

JOEY. I am so fucking angry!

SYLVIE. I feel angry at myself. I think I regret not saying anything. (*Beat.*) Because . . .

JOEY & SYLVIE. It's so fucking infuriating . . .

SYLVIE. To know he's out there just happy and living his life and stuff. And maybe even doing it to someone else . . . and that's—

JOEY. I know. (*Beat. A moment of relief for* SYLVIE *and* JOEY.)

SYLVIE. I hate him, you know?

JOEY. Yes, I know.

SYLVIE. I mean, I think what you did . . .

JOEY. Yes, I do . . . No, I do . . . I do—believe in what I'm doing—yes.

SYLVIE. (*She looks at* JOEY.) Thank you for doing it, is what I want to say.

JOEY. I just wish it were different—you know . . . I don't know—I just wish that . . .

SYLVIE. I believe you. I wanted to tell you that. (JOEY *looks at* SYLVIE.)

(*Blackout.*)

THE END

PRODUCTION NOTES

The staging of *SLUT* should be clean, simple, honest, and fast-paced. The focus is kept on the actors, the text, and the power of the story. Set elements are minimalist: a desk, a chair, and a bench. (Rehearsal blocks are effective as substitute.) There should be no attempt to design sets for each location.

After the prologue, Joey's storyline and those of girls in her community interweave, informing each other, playing side-by-side for the remainder of the play. Staging should support the intense purging of Joey's testimony, while clearly distinguishing the separate settings and character journeys for the audience. Thus, sound, light, and projections are major elements, constantly redefining the space and propelling the story forward.

Projections are a challenging undertaking but essential component of the play. As we were told by our brilliant projection designer Grant McDonald, the most important questions to ask as you begin projection design for *SLUT* are: Why does this screen exist? What is the screen? Who does it belong to? How does it fit into the set? Remember that social media and smartphones often play crucial roles in the lives of young people and the mass sharing of information. To this point, we took time to create a "homemade" video of Joey and the boys (we found volunteer actors) pregaming: "drinking," dancing, and having fun. The footage functioned as an iPhone movie uploaded to a social media platform, and video is played on the screen during the pregaming scene to provide context for the audience. Additionally, in all of our productions, we incorporated *live* video feed of Joey being interviewed, which was projected behind her onto the screen throughout the show. This effect helped add to the atmosphere of being "watched," under the community microscope, examined and distorted—as many young women experience when they come forward. To learn more about licensing the easily customizable projections used in the original National Tour of *SLUT*, please visit www.GrantMcDonald.com and click on "licensing."

Throughout the play, Joey and the others often speak to characters on the fourth wall. There should be no live actors filling those roles. The Assistant District Attorney, Jane's mom, Joey's dad, George, Luke, and Tim are not meant to have faces in any production of *SLUT*. (One exception: George,

Luke, and Tim appear briefly in the pregaming video, if you decide to create one.)

Entrances and exits should be fast and seamless. Out of necessity, we experimented with having the actors enter and exit from different places throughout the audience—signifying that all the girls in the world of the play are constantly watching Joey from the moment she comes forward. It worked well, so we kept it. Feel free to do the same.

As you have read, there are a few cultural references in the play: *Friday Night Lights*, *Frozen*, AskFM.com, *Game of Thrones*, etc. Throughout our productions of *SLUT* we've had to update these references in order for the story to stay in the *present time*—you should do the same.

SLUT tells the story of eleven females characters. The play makes most sense through the voice and eyes of teenage young women. It is important to take into account the intersectionality of race, class, etc. and how those elements impact the telling of this story. These are essential questions to the conversation around *SLUT*, as well as the script's interpretation.

The action depicted in *SLUT* is intense and can be triggering. The characters in *SLUT* are in the midst of adolescence, and sex, drugs, and drinking often dominate their conversations. The humor, vulgarity, and insecurity displayed by the characters throughout the play must be a part of the conversation. While open to adjustment suggestions/requests, no alteration of the script may be made without permission from Katie Cappiello. Contact Katie with questions: Katie@TheArtsEffectNYC.com

Finally, engaging your team in conversations about why you all are producing this show should be at the heart of your process. We encourage all involved to research the subject. Our suggestions are:

- Jennifer Baumgardner's powerful documentary *It Was Rape* (also an invaluable preparation resource for your actors in *SLUT*)
- Amy Ziering's award-winning film *The Invisible War*
- Black Women's Blueprint Truth and Reconciliation Commission
- Leora Tanenbaum's "I Am Not a Slut: Slut-Shaming in the Age of the Internet"
- www.KnowYourIX.org
- The Anti Violence Project

Consider building an advocacy campaign in conjunction with your production of *SLUT*. Find tips and resources at www.StopSlut.org. Most importantly, talk to students, classmates, parents, and friends about these issues and listen to their stories. Sexual shaming and violence touch everyone—give people a space to share, process, and heal.

PROPERTY LIST

Cell phones for all 11 characters

5 gym bags (JOEY, NATALIE, GRACE, CHRISTINA, DANIELLE)

Red Bull can (JOEY)

Makeup pouch (JOEY)

3 Laptops (JOEY, JANE, ANNA—used by other characters throughout)

Vodka bottle (JOEY)

Legal pad and pen (JOEY)

Bottle of water (JOEY)

Bagel or donut on a small paper plate (JOEY)

Twizzlers (LEILA/DANIELLE)

Box of condoms (DOMINIQUE)

Lip gloss (JULIE)

Starbucks coffee cup and cookie bag (SYLVIE)

The Feminist Press is a nonprofit educational organization founded to amplify feminist voices. FP publishes classic and new writing from around the world, creates cutting-edge programs, and elevates silenced and marginalized voices in order to support personal transformation and social justice for all people.

See our complete list of books at
feministpress.org

THE FEMINIST PRESS
AT THE CITY UNIVERSITY OF NEW YORK
FEMINISTPRESS.ORG